DOES THE U.S. NO-CONCESSIONS POLICY DETER KIDNAPPINGS OF AMERICANS?

Brian Michael Jenkins

Perspective
EXPERT INSIGHTS ON A TIMELY POLICY ISSUE

Contents

Foreword

Four Decades of Analysis and Action Frame a Centuries-Old Debate

JOHN PARACHINI
DIRECTOR, RAND CYBER AND INTELLIGENCE POLICY CENTER

The killings of American hostages by the Islamic State of Iraq and Syria in recent years reopened the question of the efficacy of the U.S. policy of not paying ransom or making other concessions to secure the release of Americans held by terrorists. In an article written for *The Hill*, a newspaper aimed at Washington lawmakers, Brian Michael Jenkins, senior adviser to RAND President Michael Rich, pointed out that the U.S. no-ransom policy dates back to a 1973 hostage situation in Khartoum, Sudan. During that incident, members of the Black September terrorist group demanded, among other things, the release of Sirhan B. Sirhan, the convicted assassin of Senator Robert F. Kennedy, and then murdered the U.S. ambassador and his deputy chief of mission (Jenkins, 2014).

Jenkins' work on the U.S. no-concessions policy began more than four decades ago and reflects a unique combination of research and personal experience. The story begins in 1972, when the U.S. Department of State asked the RAND Corporation, which had recently initiated a research program on international terrorism, to assist in developing strategies and tactics of negotiating for human life. Jenkins and members of his team fanned out across the globe to conduct detailed case studies of past terrorist hostage incidents in Argentina, Brazil, Canada, Guatemala, Haiti, Mexico, Spain, Turkey, and Uruguay. The case studies would enable researchers to distill lessons learned and catalog negotiating tactics and techniques. Because tactics depended on policy, the RAND team also looked at this broader issue (Jenkins, Ronfeldt, and Turin, 1976).

In the early 1970s, dealing with hostage incidents was a contentious subject in the State Department. Even though the deaths of the two diplomats in the Khartoum incident, which had occurred only months after RAND began its terrorism research, sealed U.S. policy in blood, many Foreign Service officers felt that if they were being assigned to countries where they would be exposed to a high risk of being kidnapped, the U.S. government should assume some responsibility for securing their release. And despite the line drawn in Khartoum, diplomats responsible for conducting negotiations in subsequent hostage situations wanted to retain some room for maneuver.[1]

Jenkins and his team did not promote a particular policy choice but, consistent with RAND's analytical approach, examined the pros and cons of three policy alternatives: a strict no-concessions policy, a flexible policy, and a policy that made safe release of the hostages the primary objective. There were several good reasons for holding to a no-concessions policy: The release of prisoners, the most common terrorist demand, would subvert the criminal justice system. Cash ransoms would be used to fund further terrorist operations. And other political concessions would raise issues of governance: Who would determine U.S. foreign policy—elected officials or terrorists holding hostages?

Proponents of the government's no-concessions policy argued that it was also an effective deterrent. However,

> Proponents of the government's no-concessions policy argued that it was also an effective deterrent. However, RAND researchers found the evidence to support this contention meager and unconvincing.

RAND researchers found the evidence to support this contention meager and unconvincing. Terrorist kidnappers most often made their demands on foreign governments, not on the United States. When their demands were not met, the terrorist kidnappers still attracted worldwide publicity and provoked government crises. And even when hostages were rescued, terrorists elsewhere chose to believe that the release was simply a cover for a negotiated payment. Different governments followed different policies, but history showed little correlation between a government's negotiating posture and the absence or occurrence of further kidnappings. This finding, Jenkins recalls, led to some frank exchanges with then–Secretary of State Henry Kissinger. A strict no-concessions stance remained U.S. policy.

Paul Austin, who, at the time, was chairman of RAND's Board of Trustees, took a personal interest in the research. Austin was also the chairman of the Coca-Cola Company, one of whose executives had recently been held for ransom by terrorists in Argentina. Shortly thereafter, two more Coca-Cola executives were kidnapped in rapid succession. With Austin's assistance, Jenkins flew to Buenos Aires and met with corporate officials. This experience gave him first-hand exposure to hostage negotiations.

In the late 1970s, Europe faced a growing problem with domestic terrorists. In 1978, members of Italy's Red Brigades kidnapped former Italian Prime Minister Aldo Moro. Jenkins' work at RAND had brought him to the attention of Italian authorities, and he was asked to assist the "brain trust" that Italy's Minister of the Interior, Francesco Cossiga, had established. Jenkins briefed the Italian Parliament's oversight committee on intelligence and consulted with its new intelligence service, *Servizio per le Informazioni e la Sicurezza Democratica.* Jenkins would later appeal personally to Cossiga, who subsequently became the president of Italy, for assistance in gaining the release of American hostages held in Lebanon.

These were Italy's "years of lead," a period of bitter armed struggle and terrorism. Political leaders were not the only people in the terrorists' sights—the Red Brigades had contemplated kidnapping the Pope, and they regularly targeted executives of Italy's large corporations, carrying out assassinations, kneecappings, and kidnappings. Jenkins was also asked to assist the Italian corporation Montedison, one of the Red Brigades' main targets.

In 1981, the Venice column of the Red Brigades kidnapped Giuseppe Taliercio, a Montedison executive. Jenkins worked with Efrem Campese, a famous former Carabiniere colonel who had become Montedison's Director of Security. Despite desperate negotiating efforts, after 47 days of captivity, Taliercio was murdered. The kidnappers left his bullet-riddled body in the trunk of a car.

The experience in this case would prove important when, six months later, the same column of the Red Brigades kidnapped U.S. GEN James Dozier. The U.S. government's counterterrorist efforts at that time were focused exclusively on international terrorism—that is, the spillover of terrorist violence into the international arena when terrorists attacked foreigners, hijacked airliners, or went abroad to carry out attacks. Italian terrorists kidnapping or killing other Italians in Italy was a domestic Italian matter. The chronology of terrorist attacks the U.S. government was using, which had been created at RAND, did not, by design, include such acts.

Because the Red Brigades had confined their violence primarily to domestic targets, the group had not been an intelligence priority in the United States, and little was known about it when General Dozier was kidnapped. Jenkins was requested to immediately begin writing a primer on the Red Brigades. The first version was completed in a few days and was followed by subsequent expanded iterations. Jenkins noted that Antonio Savasta, the leader of the Venice column, was typical of the Red Brigades' "third generation." More thug than ideologue, he knew how to plan a kidnapping but had no idea how to negotiate a satisfactory outcome. His default decision was to murder the hostage—recall that he killed Taliercio on his 47th day of captivity. That set a time frame for getting Dozier out: Italian commandos rescued the general on the 42nd day of his captivity.

In 1985, Jenkins edited and co-authored a book about kidnapping, which described some of these experiences. It was published under the title *Terrorism and Personal Protection* (Jenkins, 1984a).[2] The authors of some of the chapters are pen names of people involved in the actual cases.

Meanwhile, the focus of political kidnapping had shifted to Lebanon, where Shia Muslim extremists backed by Iran abducted nearly 100 foreigners, among them Father Martin Jenco, the local director of Catholic Relief Services (CRS) in Lebanon. Lawrence Pezzullo, a former U.S. diplomat, had recently become the president of CRS worldwide. As head of the political section at the U.S. embassy in Guatemala in 1970, he had dealt with the kidnapping of Sean Holly, the U.S. labor attaché. This was one of Jenkins' case studies, and he and Pezzullo had remained friends. Before taking the reins at CRS, Pezzullo had served as ambassador to Uruguay and Nicaragua.

When Father Jenco was kidnapped, Ambassador Pezzullo asked Jenkins to assist, as a consultant to the

Catholic Church and the liaison between CRS (and other organizations) and U.S. officials working on the case. No direct negotiations took place between CRS and the kidnappers, although numerous convincing con men emerged claiming direct lines of communication with those holding the American hostages. The Catholic Church was not willing to pay ransom, and that was not what the kidnappers wanted anyway. Holding hostages made them important players in the complicated politics of Lebanon's civil war and protected them against U.S. retaliation; they also sought the release of comrades imprisoned in Kuwait. These demands were not met, but Father Jenco was released after 18 months of captivity. It was subsequently

> It was subsequently revealed that the United States, in contravention of its own policy, had secretly sold arms to Iran in return for Iran using its influence over Iranian-supported organizations in Lebanon to bring about the release of Jenco and some of the other hostages.

revealed that the United States, in contravention of its own policy, had secretly sold arms to Iran in return for Iran using its influence over Iranian-supported organizations in Lebanon to bring about the release of Jenco and some of the other hostages.

Terry Waite, a representative of the Church of England, was also involved in international efforts to free the hostages in Lebanon until he himself was kidnapped during a trip to Beirut in January 1987. Jenkins was able to warn Anglican Church officials about a pair of particularly persuasive con artists whom he had previously encountered while working on the Jenco case. The two had already managed to bilk the Church of England for a down payment (Lion, 1988). Jenkins subsequently became a consultant to the Church of England, working with John Lyttle for five years to bring the hostages in Lebanon home. It was a frustrating saga, with futile meetings in Lebanon, Cyprus, and Istanbul. The surviving hostages were not released until 1991, just a few months after Lyttle died of a heart attack. Robin Wright, author of the acclaimed book *Sacred Rage*, and Jenkins co-authored an analysis of the Lebanon kidnappings (Jenkins and Wright, 1987).

In 1989, Jenkins left RAND to join Kroll Associates, an international investigative and security firm. As the firm's deputy chairman, he created Kroll's crisis response division, which provided assistance to corporations and families faced with ransom kidnappings, extortion threats, terrorism, and sabotage. The assistance took the form of specialized insurance services offered by AIG insurance company, for which Kroll became the official responder. Jenkins personally assisted in the response to kidnappings in Latin America and the Balkans. By this time, kidnap-and-ransom policies had become common in the insurance industry, with each insurer retaining its own dedicated team of responders. Kidnapping had become a normalized business, although the work remained difficult and sometimes dangerous.

Kroll had an exceptionally experienced team. It included Tom Clayton, a former State Department official who had personally handled several hundred kidnappings and was the model for the movie *Proof of Life,* and his son; Arish Turle, a former British Special Air Service commando and one of the founders of Control Risks, another major responder to kidnappings (he had spent months in a Colombian jail for helping to arrange a ransom payment); and Felix Batista, a former U.S. soldier and kidnapping expert who had helped negotiate many ransoms in Mexico and who later was kidnapped himself in Saltillo, Mexico, and presumably murdered. He had just given an anti-abduction seminar to a group of businessmen, and his disappearance was seen as a warning from the kidnapping rings not to resist.

During the 1990s, the Kroll team responded to a kidnapping somewhere in the world on an average of once every two weeks; at one point, it was assisting in nine ransom negotiations simultaneously. Adding extortion cases and other threats, the team responded to an incident somewhere in the world about once every 72 hours. Cell phones were just coming into use then, and team members were always on call. Jenkins recalls the time as nerve-wracking and "just a bit addictive."

Jenkins returned to RAND in 1998. Although consulted on kidnapping cases, he now prefers to steer private inquiries to others. In 2006, he co-authored a detailed analysis of the ransom kidnappings plaguing Iraq as chaos engulfed the country (Jenkins, 2006). He also continues

It is the responsibility of governments to apprehend kidnappers and destroy their organizations, whether the hostage-takers are motivated by ideology or by greed. But that does not preclude private efforts to save lives.

to serve as an adviser to Commercial Crime Services, the London-based crime-fighting arm of the International Chamber of Commerce. One of Commercial Crime Services' divisions is the International Maritime Bureau, which deals with piracy on the high seas and runs the Piracy Reporting Centre in Kuala Lumpur, Malaysia. Pirates operating out of Somalia threaten shipping in the Indian Ocean and demand ransoms for ships' crews, who may be held for months.

Jenkins believes that it should not be the policy of the U.S. government to pay ransom; however, in the interest of full disclosure, he was personally involved in cases where ransoms were paid for the safe return of hostages. Jenkins sees no contradiction in this. It is the responsibility of governments to apprehend kidnappers and destroy their organizations, whether the hostage-takers are motivated by ideology or by greed. But that does not preclude private efforts to save lives. Jenkins points out that when ransom kidnappings occur in the United States, families of kidnap victims routinely negotiate with kidnappers and pay ransoms, often with assistance from the Federal Bureau of Investigation.

Al Qaeda's affiliates and the Islamic State of Iraq and Syria, Jenkins says, are just the latest incarnations of an old business. From the 16th to the 19th centuries, Muslim pirates seized ships and raided the coasts of southern Europe, taking Christian captives, who were held for years as slaves until ransomed by their families or churches.

Friars of the Trinitarian and Mercedarian orders in Spain specialized in ransom negotiations and deliveries.

During the 17th and 18th centuries, churches in towns on the Atlantic coast of the United States also routinely raised ransoms to buy the freedom of U.S. sailors. Before the United States fought wars against the Barbary pirates, the U.S. government paid significant ransoms to the corsairs.

More than two centuries later, the payment of ransom remains a controversial issue.

Does the U.S. No-Concessions Policy Deter Kidnappings of Americans?

The persistence of the question of whether the United States should ever pay ransom to terrorists holding hostages is perhaps not remarkable. One can find historical precedents for both sides of the argument in the attempts of the newly established government of the United States to grapple with the Barbary pirates who held U.S. sailors hostage at the end of the 18th and beginning of the 19th centuries. While popular memory recalls only that the United States ultimately went to war with one of the pirate states, in fact, ransoms were privately raised and routinely paid to purchase the freedom of U.S. sailors.

Churches in Atlantic port towns regularly appealed to their congregations for what was referred to as "redemption money" to ransom those held by pirates. Sometimes, hostages died before their ransoms could be delivered, and the money was devoted to other pious purposes. In the early 18th century, unused redemption money was used to support New York's landmark Trinity Church. The U.S. government itself paid ransoms to pirates holding hostages both before the Barbary Wars and as part of a settlement after the hostilities.

Whether or not to bargain for human life is an inherently difficult question. Should government save the lives of hostages even if it risks encouraging further hostage-taking and may put more people at peril in the future? Should a few be sacrificed now in order to protect many others in the future? Moral arguments can be mustered on both sides, but it is important to consider the historical evidence about the presumptions on which policies are based.

In 1972, when the RAND Corporation initiated its research on terrorism, one of the co-sponsors of the research effort asked the project team to specifically address the issue of dealing with hostage incidents.[3] A string of kidnappings of U.S. diplomats, beginning with the September 1969 abduction of the U.S. ambassador to Brazil, made this a topic of heated debate in the U.S. Department of State. So-called hardliners took on those who sought a more flexible policy, and the debate over

Summary of Major Points

- Deterrence is offered as the principal reason for the U.S. adherence to a no-concessions policy. Logically, a no-concessions policy should be a deterrent to kidnapping. No concessions means denying a reward to the kidnappers, thereby removing the incentive to kidnap Americans.

- The deterrent effect of the no-concessions policy, however, may be eroded by the fact that kidnappers are not aware of U.S. policy, do not believe it, or may not care because other objectives will still be served by holding Americans hostage.

- The RAND Corporation's research in the early 1970s was unable to find persuasive evidence supporting the assertion that a no-concessions policy provided an effective deterrent. There was little correlation between the different negotiating policies adopted by various governments and the absence or occurrence of further kidnappings.

- Different precedents and practices—ransom payments in domestic kidnappings, payments by private parties abroad, not resisting the demands of airline hijackers (until 2001), a highly publicized breach of policy by the U.S. government itself, prisoner exchanges following or during armed conflicts, and concessions by other governments to obtain the release of U.S. hostages—have blurred perceptions of U.S. policy.

- The U.S. no-concessions policy may often be irrelevant to the kidnappers' aims. Terrorists take hostages to extract ransom or other concessions from other governments, to attract attention and make themselves important players in the region, to use the hostages as shields against government military operations, to discourage foreign investment, to create political crises that will embarrass the hostage-takers' foes, or to make demands they know will not be met, thereby giving them an excuse to murder their hostages while blaming the government for its callous obstinacy.

- The most important factor in reducing further kidnappings appears to be the fate of the kidnappers. Where they are apprehended and face stiff penalties and their gangs and groups are destroyed, kidnappings decline.

- The no-concessions policy applies to the position of the U.S. government. It was never intended to prevent private parties from negotiating and paying ransoms, which was always the practice in dealing with domestic ransom kidnappings and for Americans held abroad.

- Over the past half century, other governments have made concessions, including the release of prisoners and the payment of ransom to obtain the release of American hostages.

- Despite the U.S. no-concessions policy, U.S. citizens continue to top the list of nationalities kidnapped by terrorists. This may be explained by the prominent role and perceived influence of the United States and the ubiquity of U.S. citizens around the world. Nationals of the United Kingdom, which also has a no-concessions policy, are second on the list.

- Research by RAND and other institutions shows little evidence of nationality-specific targeting. In conflict zones, terrorists (or criminal gangs who sell hostages to terrorists) kidnap opportunistically.

- While a no-concessions policy may not deter kidnappings, it may affect the treatment of hostages in captivity and determine their ultimate fate. According to a 2015 study published by West Point, Americans held hostage by jihadist groups are nearly four times as likely to be murdered as other Western hostages (Loertscher and Milton, 2015). The no-concessions policy may be only part of the reason. Another factor would be the jihadists' intense hostility toward the United States.

- While the U.S. no-concessions policy has not deterred kidnappings, there is some evidence that political concessions and ransom payments appear to encourage further kidnappings and escalating demands.

- And although it did not produce any demonstrable decline in kidnappings of U.S. citizens, a 2016 study published in the *European Journal of Political Economy* argues that, without the no-concessions policy, there would have been even more kidnappings of U.S. nationals (Brandt, George, and Sandler, 2016).

- Finally, the no-concessions policy serves goals other than deterrence. Terrorists use ransoms to finance further operations, releasing prisoners would undermine the judicial system, and making other political concessions raises issues of governance.

U.S. policy was launched. This paper examines some of these earlier contentions and discusses what research at the time suggested.

The issue addressed here is the U.S. policy of not paying ransom to terrorists holding Americans hostage. Deterrence is offered as the principal reason for the U.S. adherence to a no-concessions policy, but whether empirical evidence supports that position remains a question.

The Need for a Tough Public Posture

In a private discussion in the early 1970s, Secretary of State William Rogers stated that the United States needed a "masculine policy" for dealing with terrorists. He said this forcefully several times, each time slamming his fist into the palm of his other hand. What he meant was that the United States could not look weak in the face of terrorism—it had to appear tough. As terrorists could seldom be attacked directly, being tough on terrorists became being tough in negotiations. If the United States could not always capture or kill terrorists, it could take a hard line in negotiations and not be shoved around, refusing to engage with them at all and rejecting any concessions.

Although it reflects frustration and emotion, being tough in negotiations has popular appeal to a U.S. audience. Whatever the United States does to bring back hostages, it must appear firm, resolute, and unyielding. No-negotiations and no-concessions policies fit an American narrative. Over the years, paying ransom to redeem hostages from a terrible captivity—once considered a noble goal, a religious duty—has come to be portrayed as dishonorable, a display of weakness, and certainly not a masculine policy. This has led to some mythologizing about past incidents.

Americans admire Israel's toughness in dealing with terrorists and its daring rescues of hostages, forgetting that, over the years, Israel has released thousands of prisoners in exchange for the release of a much smaller number of Israelis or other nationals, including Americans, held hostage by terrorists.

Tough rhetoric is more readily recalled than the little-known, creative, behind-the-scenes diplomacy and concessions, sometimes encouraged by the United States but made by others, to bring Americans home. The no-concessions policy thus acquires an aura of effectiveness that is not easily supported by empirical evidence.

As I have repeated many times, "terrorism is theater." Terrorists choreograph violence or threats of violence to create an atmosphere of fear and alarm, which causes people to exaggerate the strength and reach of the terrorists and the magnitude of the threat they pose. It works both ways—responding to terrorism also has an element of theater. It is difficult for governments to dismiss the terrorist threat while at the same time summoning the vigilance required and mobilizing the resources necessary to combat the terrorists. But appearing competent, in control, and implacable reduces unreasoning fear and therefore is an important antidote to terror.

This paper addresses one aspect of a particular policy (the no-concessions policy). It is not an argument for or against the policy. It is about the difficult analysis of indirect empirical evidence, recognizing that policies also reflect political realities. Hostage incidents are inherently dangerous to political leadership. Lives hang in the balance. The government may be thrown into crisis, but it cannot appear callous or craven. Although hostage deaths can be a political disaster, concessions will be denounced. Each case is different. Policies provide guidelines, not prescriptions.

Deterrence Is Only One of Several Goals

It is important to remember that deterrence is only one of several goals of the U.S. no-concessions policy. Such a policy prevents governments in countries where a kidnapping occurs from ducking their responsibility to protect foreign diplomats and other nationals within their borders and leaving the governments of the hostages to solve the problem. This was the original purpose of the U.S. policy.

But there are other benefits to a no-concessions policy. For instance, the payment of cash ransoms provides funds for further terrorist operations, so refusing to pay avoids that support. Instead of viewing a ransom payment as a cash amount, one can think of it as the number of AK-47s the money would buy at the going market rate to get an idea of what this might mean to terrorist kidnappers. Expressing ransom payments in the currency of future violence challenges the humanitarian imperative to save the life of the individual hostage.

Making concessions to terrorists raises issues of governance. At some point, it becomes a question of who runs the country—terrorists holding hostages or the country's elected officials?

In addition, the U.S. policy precludes other concessions to terrorists holding hostages. The release of terrorist prisoners in return for the release of hostages is one of the most common demands, but releasing prisoners subverts the criminal justice system and may put dangerous individuals at large. Moreover, making concessions to terrorists, especially releasing prisoners or yielding to other political demands, raises issues of governance. At some point, it becomes a question of who runs the country—terrorists holding hostages or the country's elected officials?

Whatever value a policy has (or lacks) as a deterrent, the alternative of readily yielding to terrorists holding hostages appears to encourage repetition of the tactic. Although I am admittedly on soft ground here, the evidence that making concessions incentivizes kidnappings appears stronger than the evidence that not making concessions deters kidnappings. At least, we can find evidence of further kidnappings where kidnappers' demands are routinely met—absent effective law enforcement. Evidence of deterrence is much harder to identify, especially where law enforcement is not effective. I will return to this point.

Over time, the objective of U.S. policy seems to have shifted—first, from avoiding being pulled into direct negotiations, then to deterring kidnappings, and now to denying terrorists material support. This evolution of policy mirrors the changes in U.S. views of combating terrorism.

In the early 1970s, when the policy for dealing with terrorism was being formulated, the United States framed the problem as one of outlawing terrorist tactics. The United States did not directly counterattack foreign terrorist groups—that was a local responsibility—but instead sought merely to prevent local conflicts from spilling over into the international arena in the form of terrorist attacks. The intent was to build international consensus to outlaw terrorism, making terrorism a criminal activity and a violation of the rules of war, regardless of political cause. The State Department took the lead.

The United States gradually reframed this policy, putting greater emphasis on directly attacking designated terrorist groups by reducing their cash flow and, when necessary, attacking them directly with military force. In this context, the objective of U.S. policy on ransom shifted to denying terrorists all possible sources of material support.[4]

How U.S. Policy Came About

Before examining the deterrent effect of the no-concessions policy, it is necessary to go back and understand how the policy came about. As is often the case in government, the formulation of the policy was not based on a review of alternative policy options; it emerged from the response to specific events.

In the first kidnapping of a U.S. diplomat—the abduction of Charles Burke Elbrick, the U.S. ambassador to Brazil, in September 1969—the United States took the position that it was the responsibility of the host government to protect diplomats accredited to it. That meant doing whatever was necessary to bring about their safe release if they were kidnapped. Before hearing the U.S. position, the government of Brazil had already decided to yield to the demands of the kidnappers, and it released the 15 prisoners they demanded in exchange for the release of the ambassador. This pattern continued in several subsequent cases. With tacit U.S. approval, the governments of Guatemala, the Dominican Republic, Haiti, and Mexico

> The objective of U.S. policy on ransom shifted to denying terrorists all possible sources of material support.

all released prisoners to bring about the safe return of U.S. diplomats.

This pattern changed when Uruguay's urban guerrillas, the Tupamaros, kidnapped Dan Mitrione, the American head of the Office of Public Safety in Montevideo, in 1970 and demanded the release of 150 prisoners in exchange for his release. The widely accepted history of this event is that the Uruguayan government, with U.S. backing, refused to meet the kidnappers' demands, and Mitrione was murdered. The true story differs. It is true that the government of Uruguay resisted meeting the terrorists' demands for the release of the prisoners, fearing that doing so would expose it to a coup by military hardliners. That made negotiations between Washington and Montevideo extremely delicate. While U.S. representatives urged Uruguay to make all efforts to save Mitrione's life—including negotiations, amnesties for prisoners whose release the kidnappers demanded, and the payment of ransom—the State Department also realized that concessions could prompt the overthrow of the Uruguayan government. A primary concern of the United States was ensuring that Uruguay would not throw up its hands and make securing Mitrione's release a U.S. problem.

In other words, it was not deterrence but rather preventing a foreign government from abdicating its role and dragging the United States into direct negotiations with the kidnappers that was the primary objective of U.S. policy at that time and that underpinned its later no-concessions policy. A little known fact, however, is that, when confronted with Uruguay's obstinacy, the United States considered paying a ransom thinly disguised as a reward for information. This was not going to happen, however; ten days after the kidnapping, the Tupamaros killed Mitrione. Following his death, the United States publicly denied that it had exerted any pressure on Uruguay (Ronfeldt, 1987). Many years after the Mitrione kidnapping, classified U.S. diplomatic cables were published indicating that, in a last desperate attempt to save the diplomat's life, the U.S. government urged the government of Uruguay to warn the kidnappers that if Mitrione was murdered, the government would execute prominent

The U.S. policy of refusing to make concessions to terrorist kidnappers was sealed in blood in March 1973 when two U.S. diplomats were taken hostage in Khartoum, Sudan.

Tupamaro prisoners that it held (Osorio and Marianna Enamoneta, 2010).

In the following year, urban guerrillas in Turkey, emulating those in Latin America, kidnapped four U.S. airmen. The kidnappers demanded the public broadcast of an anti-American manifesto and the payment of $400,000 in ransom in return for the airmen's release. Turkey rejected any demands beyond broadcasting a summary of the manifesto and asked the United States to support its decision (Krahenbuhl, 1977).

Attitudes in Washington were hardening, not as a result of any policy review but rather because of proliferating kidnappings and hijackings. The U.S. government informed Turkish officials that the United States would not pay ransoms, nor would it compel the Turkish government to do so. The only difference between the two governments arose over communications. U.S. officials in Ankara did not equate the Turkish government's no-concessions policy with no communications. Embassy officials communicated with the press in an effort to shape public opinion and at least indirectly communicate with the kidnappers. (The distinction between no concessions, no negotiations, and no communications has continued to be an issue of debate in the U.S. government.) The episode ended when the kidnappers, fearing that they were about to be surrounded, freed their hostages and fled. In this case, the United States endorsed Turkey's no-concessions policy.

The U.S. policy of refusing to make concessions to terrorist kidnappers was sealed in blood in March 1973 when two U.S. diplomats were taken hostage in Khartoum, Sudan, by the terrorist group Black September. The terrorists initially demanded the release of Palestinian prisoners held by Israel, members of the Baader-Meinhof terrorist gang held in Germany, and Sirhan B. Sirhan, the man who shot and killed Senator Robert F. Kennedy in 1968.

The United States was willing to talk to the terrorists and dispatched the Undersecretary of State to Khartoum, but the White House could not be seen to even be contemplating the release of the convicted assassin of President John F. Kennedy's brother, a former attorney general and senator and a Democratic presidential candidate at the time he was killed. President Richard M. Nixon made this clear when he was asked at a press conference about the demand to release Sirhan. He responded, "As far as the United States as a government giving in to blackmail demands, we cannot do so and we will not do so." News of the President's remarks was broadcast in the Middle East, where the terrorists heard it. Hours later, they murdered the two Americans, along with a Belgian official. The response to a specific question in specific circumstances became general policy. It has been U.S. policy not to make concessions to terrorists ever since.

Different Precedents and Traditions

In considering how to respond to the wave of terrorist kidnappings that spread across the world in the 1970s, U.S. officials drew on different precedents to guide policy.

Ordinary ransom kidnappings. The U.S. no-concessions policy dealt specifically with hostages held by *terrorist* kidnappers. Ransoms were usually paid in ordinary criminal ransom kidnappings in the United States, but this was not seen as a precedent for U.S. policy for dealing with terrorist hostage incidents abroad, nor was the U.S. no-concessions policy expected to change the policy for dealing with nonterrorist kidnappings. (However, there were some tensions between the State Department and the Federal Bureau of Investigation [FBI] concerning the management of hostage situations.)

Ransom demands on private parties abroad. When kidnappers abducted U.S. citizens abroad—often corporate executives—and demanded ransoms from private parties, usually their families or employers, the incidents were viewed in the context of U.S. domestic kidnappings, and the U.S. government did not interfere with negotiations or payments.

The Department of State's 2006 *Foreign Affairs Manual and Handbook* describes the U.S. posture in such circumstances: "The United States strongly urges U.S. companies and private citizens not to pay ransom. . . . If they wish to follow a path different from that of U.S. Government policy, they do so without the approval or cooperation of the U.S. Government." Also, "the U.S. Government cannot participate in developing and implementing a ransom strategy." And where private parties insist on doing so, "U.S. Foreign Service posts will limit their participation to basic administrative services, such as facilitating contacts with host government officials" (U.S. Department of State, 2006). Note that the manual says nothing about the government prohibiting or interfering with private ransom negotiations or payments.

Airline hijackings. Responses to airline hijackings drew on different protocols. Protecting the lives of the passengers remained the paramount objective. Hijackers usually demanded a change of destination, and the standard response was to comply. No one contemplated rejecting hijackers' demands. Hijackers would be dealt with after the plane had safely landed and the passengers were released. In hijackings abroad, U.S. diplomatic efforts aimed at ensuring that the hijackers were prosecuted

> While historical precedents dictated different responses in different circumstances, the result was confusion and blurred perceptions of U.S. policy.

or extradited to a country where they would be prosecuted. Policy conflicts arose when terrorist hijackers took over planes to make political demands. Making political demands changed the way the policies were perceived. Would the safety of the passengers or upholding the new no-concessions policy take precedence? Passenger safety always took precedence until the terrorist attacks on September 11, 2001. The prospect of a hijacked airliner hurtling toward a skyscraper forced the government to consider extraordinary measures, including shooting the plane down, even if this meant death for all those on board.

In cases subsequent to 1973, most hostages were released, while U.S. policy remained intact because other governments or private parties made concessions. For example, in 1976, when Croatian separatists hijacked a U.S. airliner and demanded the publication of their manifesto in five newspapers, the newspapers chose to comply. The government did not interfere.

In 1985, terrorists forced a hijacked U.S. airliner to land in Lebanon and demanded, among other things, the release of more than 700 prisoners held by Israel. This led to weeks of intense diplomacy and partial hostage releases before all the hostages were finally released, except one who had been murdered by the hijackers. U.S. policy emerged intact: It had not directly negotiated with the terrorists, and it had made no concessions other than a promise before the final release of hostages that it would not retaliate against Lebanon for the incident. However, during the negotiations, Israel released some of the prisoners while claiming that the release was unrelated to the hijacking; after the last hostages were released, Israel released 700 more prisoners.

Prisoner exchanges. The U.S. no-concessions policy did not alter the long-standing practice of prisoner exchanges following hostilities in order to bring American prisoners of war home. The no-concessions policy was never intended to change this practice, even when the captors were insurgent groups. For example, the Viet Cong, which was part of the negotiations that led to the release of American prisoners of war in 1973, and, years later, the Taliban, which continued to fight against U.S. forces as insurgents after being overthrown by the United States in 2001, were not designated by the United States as terrorist groups. This was important for understanding the later exchange of Taliban prisoners for U.S. SSGT Bowe Bergdahl.

Blurred Perceptions of Policy

While historical precedents dictated different responses in different circumstances, the result was confusion and blurred perceptions of U.S. policy. The U.S. government would not make concessions to terrorists holding hostages, but it would not publicly denounce or interfere with negotiations by other governments or their making of concessions to win the release of American hostages. Nor would the U.S. government interfere with press coverage, including the broadcast of press conferences with terrorist hostage-takers or decisions by U.S. newspapers to publish terrorist manifestos to bring about the release of hostages. This was freedom of the press, and publicity was viewed as an acceptable "concession."

The United States would also not interfere with private parties paying ransom to kidnappers holding Americans hostage, even when it became clear that the kidnappers were members of terrorist organizations. This was considered a private affair. It was not until recently that some U.S. officials began to consider this to be a violation of the statute prohibiting material support to terrorist organizations. At least two families of U.S. hostages held in Syria by the Islamic State of Iraq and Syria (ISIS) were warned that they could be prosecuted if they attempted to privately negotiate a ransom payment.[5] However, U.S. Department of Justice officials have stated that they would not prosecute families for paying ransom to terrorist kidnappers and that they have never contemplated doing so.

When President Barack Obama announced on June 24, 2015, that the United States was not going to prosecute families of hostages for paying ransom, some in the press reported that news as the United States would "no longer prosecute." In other words, they reported that this was a change in policy, when, in fact, the President merely confirmed two aspects of existing policy—the U.S. government would not pay ransom but it would not prosecute families for doing so.

The U.S. government would not try to prevent hijackers from changing the destinations of hijacked aircraft or interfere with the payment of cash ransoms to criminal hijackers in the United States, but the government itself would not make concessions to terrorists. The United States would not release prisoners in exchange for hostages held by terrorists but would exchange prisoners with governments and nongovernment adversaries in wartime situations.

Terrorists may not understand the distinctions the United States makes among terrorist kidnappings where its no-concessions policy applies; its perceived obligation to bring U.S. soldiers home, including by exchanging prisoners; its willingness to let other governments make concessions to obtain the release of American hostages; and its hands-off approach to private negotiations and ransom payments. These distinctions make sense only in the context of the United States' own historical experience. From the outside, they may be seen as inconsistencies. Contradictory and sometimes simply erroneous public statements by U.S. officials further contribute to the confusion.

The Logic of Deterrence

Logically, a no-concessions policy should be a deterrent to kidnapping. No concessions means denying a reward to the kidnappers, thereby removing the incentive to kidnap Americans. Unrewarded behavior is unlikely to be repeated, or so the argument runs. This might be the case for criminal kidnappers who seek only cash, but simply removing one kind of reward does not mean that terrorists, who also have political objectives, could not still obtain other kinds of rewards through kidnappings. I will return to these nonfinancial rewards later.

Theoretically, there are many reasons why a no-concessions policy might not deter kidnappings. The kidnappers simply might not know about U.S. policy. They might not believe U.S. policy—that is, they might think that, despite public declarations to the contrary, when faced with an actual event, the United States will give in. Or the kidnappers might consider U.S. policy irrelevant to their goals.

The Kidnappers Might Not Know About or Understand U.S. Policy

Ignorance about U.S. policy could account for some kidnappings. According to the Global Terrorism Database (GTD) maintained by the National Consortium for the Study of Terrorism and Responses to Terrorism (START) at the University of Maryland, 356 U.S. nationals were kidnapped between January 1970 and December 2016 (START, undated). Eighteen of these kidnappings were carried out by remote tribal groups or by individuals, some of whom were mentally or emotionally impaired, rather than by terrorist organizations. It is unlikely that these kidnappers understood U.S. policy.

The Kidnappers Might Not Believe U.S. Policy Statements

U.S. officials have cited anecdotal evidence that terrorists were aware of and were deterred by U.S. policy, but other anecdotal evidence suggests that some terrorists believe that hostage rescues or escapes were disguised deals. Even if the United States refuses to make concessions, terrorists may still expect to receive some sort of ransom from families, corporations, or other private sources.

The intended deterrent effect of the U.S. no-concessions policy is further blurred by the fact that the United States appears to have violated it at times. In the 1980s, the Ronald Reagan administration secretly sold arms to Iran, which, in return, was expected to use its influence to bring about the release of American hostages held by its Shia protégés in Lebanon. As arms went to Iran, individual hostages were released (although more people were also kidnapped, giving the hostage-takers a "bank account" of hostages to trade). The secret trading of arms for hostages was exposed in late 1986 and caused a damaging political scandal, even more so when it was revealed that the Reagan administration had used profits from the arms sales to secretly fund the Contra rebels in Nicaragua, which Congress had expressly prohibited.

The 2014 release of an American hostage held by a jihadist group in Syria also lends itself to the inference that a deal was done. Peter Theo Curtis, a U.S. journalist, was kidnapped and held for 22 months by Jabhat al-Nusra, al Qaeda's affiliate in Syria. His release was negotiated by the government of Qatar. No explanation for his release was given. All parties involved, including Curtis's family, the U.S. government, and the Qatari government, denied that any ransom was paid, although the Qatari government reportedly had been involved in brokering several ransom payments to obtain the release of European hostages. This fueled public speculation that the terrorists holding Curtis got something in return for his release (Foster, 2014).

The Kidnappers Might Not Care About U.S. Policy

The kidnappers' indifference to U.S. policy seems to be the most important reason that a no-concessions policy might not deter kidnappings. Of the 356 kidnappings of U.S. nationals in START's GTD, 118 were carried out by unknown perpetrators. Although included as terrorist incidents, these appear to be mostly the actions of criminal gangs seeking cash ransom. Whether the ransom is paid by private parties or the U.S. government makes no difference to them.

The distinction between terrorist and ordinary criminal kidnappers is sometimes difficult to make. Inspired by sensational ransoms reportedly paid to terrorist groups, criminal gangs take the field, sometimes pretending to be terrorist groups in order to increase their leverage. There also have been cases in which members of guerrilla or terrorist groups engaging in kidnapping have "moonlighted" to support or enrich themselves.

Terrorists may kidnap Americans in order to make demands on the local government or on governments other than that of the United States, relying on U.S. influence or the importance of the United States to ensure that their demands will be met. In these circumstances, U.S. policy is irrelevant. Even when demands are directed at the local government, terrorists holding American hostages can still indirectly involve the United States in negotiations, thereby revealing the power and influence of the United States over the local government, which they can then portray as a puppet of the United States.

In some cases, terrorists may hold and ultimately kill American hostages to demonstrate their conviction and attract recruits or to increase their leverage over other nations whose nationals they hold. For example, ISIS advertises atrocities—beheadings, the burning of hostages, mass executions—to demonstrate its authenticity. Some of its hostages may be ransomed, and others may be selected for brutal executions. In the case of kidnappings in the private sector, where the hostage-takers hold many captives, there is always the concern that the kidnappers will kill

> In some cases, terrorists may hold and ultimately kill American hostages to demonstrate their conviction and attract recruits or to increase their leverage over other nations whose nationals they hold.

some of their hostages to underscore their determination and to increase psychological pressure on the remaining parties to pay the ransom quickly.

Terrorists also seize hostages to obtain publicity. Terrorist kidnappings to achieve this goal are almost always successful. Terrorists take hostages to cause alarm, which causes people to inflate the kidnappers' importance. The kidnappings create complicated and politically dangerous crises for the government of the hostages; the government on which the demands are made; and, in some cases, the government of the country in which the kidnapping occurs. Terrorists demonstrate their power by forcing governments to publicly make life-and-death decisions.

Terrorists may make demands that they know will not be met to give them an excuse to murder their hostages and then try to blame an obstinate government, which they can then portray as uncaring, cruel, and ultimately responsible for the bloodshed. Terrorists can carry out kidnappings in order to discourage foreign intervention, investment, assistance, or missionary activities. Terrorists can use hostages as shields against government bombing or other military actions. Terrorists can obtain status by holding hostages, which elevates the group over its terrorist rivals and makes it a factor that must be taken into account by the United States and other international actors. These goals can all be achieved whether or not the government makes concessions.

Thus, these are some of the reasons why a no-concessions policy should be, but may not always be, a deterrent.

The Empirical Evidence

Now, let's look at the empirical evidence for or against the effectiveness of a no-concessions policy. What do the numbers tell us? The historical evidence is thin.

To begin with, terrorist kidnappings are statistically rare events, making it difficult to clearly discern the effects of no-concessions policies. Other factors also complicate the analysis. The recurrence or absence of further kidnapping events under any existing policy may be affected by the fate of the kidnappers or of the kidnapping organization. The kidnappers may be apprehended or their groups may be destroyed, in which case the absence of further kidnappings has nothing to do with policy. As previously pointed out, it is not always clear whose policy or which policy applies in specific circumstances. The United States may uphold its no-concessions policy while a local government makes concessions to bring about the release of American hostages—clearly not a victory for no concessions. And, as mentioned before, deals may be disguised.

The history of kidnappings involving Americans shows no clear patterns. Turning again to the GTD listing of 356 U.S. citizens kidnapped between 1970 and 2016, we see that

- from 1970 to 1979, there were 78 kidnappings
- from 1980 to 1989, there were 66 kidnappings
- from 1990 to 1999, there were 118 kidnappings (data for 1993 are missing from the START database)
- from 2000 to 2009, there were 48 kidnappings
- from 2010 to 2016, there were 46 kidnappings.

The annual totals range from one to 19. The average annual number of kidnappings over the 47 years is eight. These very small numbers make it difficult to draw conclusions with a high degree of confidence.

With that important caveat in mind, there are some more-detailed inquiries that can be made here. For example, is it possible to discern any effect of the declaration of a no-concessions policy in 1973? I would hypothesize that there was no effect, because in some of the subsequent prominent kidnappings, local governments made concessions with or without U.S. encouragement, thus blurring the message. Moreover, since the public announcement of the policy in 1973, terrorists have seized American hostages on hundreds of occasions. The difficulty with measuring deterrence statistics is that one could speculate that, had the United States not adopted a no-concessions policy, many more would have been kidnapped. This was the question examined in more-recent research described later in this paper.

But perhaps the cash ransoms paid by private parties are contaminating the data. What would the data look like if these cash ransom cases were stripped out? It would be useful to know in how many cases demands were made on the United States as opposed to being made on other governments or private parties. It also would be useful to know the number of cases in which concessions were made to free American hostages despite U.S. policy.

The geographical pattern of the kidnappings appears to follow the general pattern of terrorist activity. Latin American groups were responsible for 41 of the 78 terrorist kidnappings in the 1970s, when many urban guerrilla groups were active. (After the initial round of political kidnappings between 1969 and 1974, most of the subsequent kidnappings were carried out by urban guerrilla groups for cash ransom.) Kidnappings in Lebanon dominate the data in the 1980s. (The START data show Colombia as the leading location, but the data appear to be incomplete.) Kidnappings in Colombia dominated in the 1990s, followed by Guatemala, Mexico, and Brazil. These were mainly cash ransom kidnappings carried out by terrorists or ordinary criminals, some of whom pretended to be terrorists.

In the first decade of the 21st century, most of the terrorist kidnappings were carried out by jihadist or insurgent groups in Iraq and Afghanistan—both conflict zones. Most of the more recent kidnappings have occurred in the Middle East, particularly Syria and Iraq, although terrorist kidnappings occurred in North Africa.

Does a policy of making concessions make nationals of a country with that policy more-attractive targets? Theoretically, it should, but the available evidence shows no correlation between national policies on concessions and the nationalities of hostages.

The START database shows that, in addition to the U.S. nationals who were kidnapped between 1970 and 2016, United Kingdom (UK) nationals were targeted in 149 cases, French citizens in 143 cases, and German citizens in 108 cases. The United States and the United Kingdom, the two countries with the clearest no-concessions policies, lead the list of targets; Americans are still the number one target of terrorist kidnappers.

France and Germany, the two countries presumed to regularly pay ransoms, were targeted in fewer cases, but this may simply reflect the ubiquity of U.S. and UK nationals abroad, opposition to the foreign policies of the two countries, the fact that there are fewer French or German nationals in some areas, or other factors. Geography is important. More French citizens may be kidnapped in North Africa simply because there are more of them in that area than other nationals. However, the case cannot be made that other nationalities are being kidnapped more frequently because their governments reportedly pay ransom.

An additional caveat is that the available data need to be carefully examined on a case-by-case basis to validate the inclusion of cases as relevant. Much information is also unavailable from existing databases. It is not clear what percentage of the total volume of kidnappings is currently documented, and important details about individual episodes are lacking.

The available evidence shows no correlation between national policies on concessions and the nationalities of hostages.

More research may be warranted on the geographic distribution of the kidnappings by nationality. Although data are hard to come by, a more detailed analysis of the presumed ransom payments by certain European governments would also be useful for understanding the magnitude of *actual* ransom payments, as opposed to the much higher ransom demands. It also would be useful to know the number of cases in which governments are believed to have arranged ransoms to free their nationals, as opposed to truly private payments made to free kidnapped corporate executives.

It appears that terrorists often kidnap victims with little regard to their nationality, and in some countries, criminal gangs may kidnap anyone they can and then "sell" the hostages to terrorist groups, which will find ways to exploit them. As pointed out previously, ISIS holds hostages of several nationalities and exploits them in different ways. In such cases, government policies on the issue of

Confronted by a government hard line but able to coerce corporations to pay huge ransoms, terrorists changed their targets from government officials to corporate executives.

concessions may be a greater factor in determining the fate of the hostages than any original selection criteria.

One thing that is clear is that kidnappings of foreign nationals, and specifically U.S. nationals, represent only a tiny fraction of the total volume of criminal and political kidnappings that occur in some of the most affected countries. Lebanon during its civil war; Colombia since the early 1980s; Iraq since the U.S. occupation; and Mexico, Brazil, the Philippines, and Syria today have all suffered high levels of criminal activity, with thousands of kidnappings. In some years, more than 2,000 individuals were kidnapped in Colombia alone. Most of the American hostages have been taken in these conflict zones and high-crime areas, often for cash ransoms. The U.S. no-concessions policy thus affects only a sliver of a vast kidnapping industry.

Although it is difficult to discern the deterrent effects of government no-concessions policies, it appears that the willingness of families and corporations to pay cash ransoms may have, in some cases, encouraged further ransom kidnappings. Coupled with government no-concessions policies, this may have created a diversionary instead of a deterrent effect; that is, confronted by a government hard line but able to coerce corporations to pay huge ransoms, terrorists changed their targets from government officials to corporate executives.

The Argentine government adopted a hardline policy in responding to the first terrorist kidnappings in the country. The urban guerrilla groups switched to making demands on corporations, at first demanding that the corporations finance distributions of food to the poor or other philanthropic causes, later demanding cash payments. Ransom demands in Argentina quickly escalated from tens of thousands of dollars to hundreds of thousands, and then to millions and to tens of millions. The problem continued until the terrorist groups were destroyed in the so-called "dirty war" that lasted from 1974 until 1983. This was a brutal campaign of oppression targeting not just the terrorist organizations, as the Argentine government claimed, but aimed at destroying all opposition to the military regime.

Ransom kidnappings were far more effective than other means of financing terrorist operations. Uruguay's Tupamaros kidnapped for political reasons but raised money the old-fashioned way by robbing banks. It took them roughly 30 bank robberies to raise $1 million, whereas Argentina's urban guerrillas could bring in that much and more by a single kidnapping.

Ransom kidnappings became a principal means of financing terrorist groups in Argentina and Colombia, later in Italy, and more recently by al Qaeda's affiliates in North Africa and Yemen. This raised the question of whether ransom payments should be outlawed altogether. The United States did not outlaw them. Italy and Colombia did so for a while, but with little apparent effect. The United Kingdom has recently prohibited the sale of kidnap and ransom insurance to discourage private ransom payments.

Outlawing ransom payments might simply drive negotiations underground while criminalizing the actions of some of the victims of terrorist demands—the families attempting to save loved ones. It would be difficult to prosecute these families, and many people would find such a law morally repugnant.

However, while readiness to pay ransoms may inspire further ransom kidnappings, such kidnappings do not happen where kidnappers are routinely apprehended,

convicted, and severely punished. Criminal kidnappings proliferate where law enforcement is weak and the probability of apprehension, conviction, and punishment is extremely low.

RAND's Early Research on Hostage Situations

When the RAND Corporation began its research on hostage situations, researchers examined specific hostage cases and looked at the effects of different government responses. These early historical studies, which were summarized in a 1975 report (Jenkins and Strauch, 1975), did not find persuasive empirical evidence to support the presumption that a no-concessions policy was an effective deterrent to kidnappings. (A more detailed discussion of these inquiries can be found in the appendix.)

The authors noted that, while different countries followed different policies, it was hard to link the absence of further kidnappings with policies regarding concessions. Brazil made concessions; Uruguay did not. The government of Argentina did not make concessions, but corporations routinely paid huge ransoms to the country's urban guerrillas. Foreign corporations withdrew their expatriates, but kidnappers continued to target local employees for whom the companies were equally obliged to negotiate. The first kidnappings prompted increased security measures in all three countries, but this appears to have had little effect; kidnappings continued. By the mid-1970s, however, the number of kidnappings had declined in all three countries (Jenkins and Strauch, 1975).

Suppression of the kidnapping organizations, not policies on concessions, appeared to be the most powerful factor in the decline of kidnappings, although this was not an endorsement of the brutal methods adopted by these governments. Likewise, in Europe, where governments more often operated within the law, it was the destruction of the kidnapping groups, not the policy pronouncements, that ended the abductions.

In the United States, ransoms were routinely paid to kidnappers, but the high probability of apprehension, conviction, and severe punishment reduced the volume of kidnappings by ordinary criminals. U.S. domestic terrorist groups, with a single exception, did not adopt the tactic. In contrast, in countries where kidnappers run little risk of arrest and conviction, ransom kidnapping remains a serious problem.

Recent Research on Kidnappings

How do the findings of the earlier RAND research hold up to the conclusions of recent research? Several recent studies examine more-recent kidnappings and the effects of different national policies. These include a study of kidnapping across time and among jihadist organizations, published in 2015 by West Point's Combating Terrorism Center (CTC); a study of the adverse effects of making concessions to kidnappers, published in 2016 in the *European Journal of Political Economy*; and an examination of Western hostage policies, published in 2017 by New America.

2015 Study of Kidnapping Across Time and Among Jihadist Organizations

The CTC report *Held Hostage: Analyses of Kidnapping Across Time and Among Jihadist Organizations* offers a detailed analysis of recent ransom kidnappings and reinforces some of the observations derived from earlier research (Loertscher and Milton, 2015). While the authors, Seth Loertscher and Daniel Milton, do not discuss the issue of policy, they agree with the observation that, between 1970 and 2013, the overwhelming majority of kidnappings were domestic (intrastate); kidnappings of Westerners were rare in the total universe of kidnappings.

My earlier research identified nationals of the United States and the United Kingdom as the most frequently targeted victims. Loertscher and Milton list Turkey, the United States, Italy, the United Kingdom, France, and Germany as the principal targets of jihadist kidnapping between 2001 and 2015 but point out that this is an anomaly. First, the database created by the authors includes Western hostages taken by pirates; those incidents were not included in the research described in this paper. Second, the prominence of Turkish nationals is the result of two incidents involving 77 hostages. The inclusion of pirates also increases Turkey's total. Many of the kidnap victims were Turkish truck drivers kidnapped in Iraq. Similarly, Italy's prominence is driven, in part, by a single incident in which 22 Italian citizens were kidnapped in Niger by the Revolutionary Armed Forces of the Sahara. If these outlier events were excluded, the United States would rank first in total kidnapping victims, followed by Turkey, the United Kingdom, France, Italy, and Germany—close to the ranking in the present paper, with the exception of the continued prominence of Turkey owing to abductions in Iraq. More detailed analysis needs to be conducted on this topic.

Loertscher and Milton (2015, p. 26) conclude that the data do not provide strong support for the idea of nationality-specific targeting:

> While several of the top six countries have seen higher kidnapping rates during this period [2001–

2015] (Turkey, Italy, and Germany), these increases do not appear to be very different from the general trend. It is interesting that France, a nation often criticized in the media for paying ransoms, has not seen a discernible increase in kidnappings. While it is possible that kidnappings that end in ransoms encourage terrorist groups to expand their operations more broadly, our data do not provide much support to the idea that nation-specific targeting is happening across the jihadist spectrum. What seems more likely is that the increase in jihadist kidnappings is a function of increased target availability or an expansion by jihadists of their zones of operation.

This would reinforce the point made here that terrorists kidnap opportunistically—and thus government policies have little effect. Loertscher and Milton reach the same conclusion:

> While nationality appears to be important in determining the fate of individuals once kidnapped, it does not appear to influence who gets kidnapped. Although kidnappings are often thought of as preplanned events against specific individuals, they often seem to occur opportunistically against individuals who are in the wrong place at the wrong time. (Loertscher and Milton, 2015, p. vii)

Earlier, I argued that government policies on concessions may be a greater factor in determining the fate of hostages than any original selection criteria. Loertscher and Milton agree. They note that "the execution rate for Americans held hostage by these [jihadist] groups is 47%; nearly four times the rate (12%) for other Western hostages" (Loertscher and Milton, 2015, p. vii). Here, I would say that the U.S. no-concessions policy may be only part

Exacting vengeance and demoralizing their U.S. foes are primary objectives of the jihadist kidnappers.

of the reason. A major factor would be the intense hostility of the jihadists toward the United States. The period examined in the CTC report encompasses the wars in Iraq and Afghanistan and the beginning of the U.S. bombing of ISIS. Exacting vengeance and demoralizing their U.S. foes are primary objectives of the jihadist kidnappers.

Loertscher and Milton also note that captors murder 32 percent of the UK citizens taken by jihadist groups. Because the UK government also rejects concessions, policy may have something to do with the high rate, although the United Kingdom was a major participant in the war in Afghanistan and also participated in the invasion of Iraq and the military campaign against ISIS. If we look at nonjihadist kidnappings, then only 6 percent of hostages from the United Kingdom are murdered. A closer examination of the data is required, but some of these cases are kidnappings by groups outside of the Middle East seeking cash ransom, which private parties provide.

The implications for policy are significant, as Loertscher and Milton indicate. The finding that U.S. citizens are four times more likely to be executed and at least four times less likely to be released than individuals from other nations is important. Additional findings of similar rates of execution and release for the United Kingdom, reversed trends for Turkey and Italy, and comparatively high release rates for France and Germany make the finding regarding U.S. citizens even more striking. It is possible that jihadist groups' perception of the United States as a global superpower supporting "apostate" regimes in the Middle East and North Africa plays a role in the high execution and low release rates of U.S. citizens. France, however, has a similar reputation among jihadist groups, yet its citizens experience significantly higher rates of release. It should be noted that, despite denials from their governments, many European countries have been identified in multiple open-source news articles as paying ransoms to jihadist groups. If this is true, it would provide a plausible explanation for their high release rates relative to the United States and the United Kingdom, which, according to public statements and open-source reporting, do not pay ransoms (Loertscher and Milton, 2015, p. 41).

The detailed research reflected in the CTC report merits additional attention.

2016 Study of the Adverse Effects of Making Concessions to Kidnappers

In a 2012 speech at Chatham House in London, David S. Cohen, the U.S. Undersecretary for Terrorism and Financial Intelligence, said,

> We know that hostage takers looking for ransoms distinguish between those governments that pay ransoms and those that do not . . . . And recent kidnapping for ransom trends appear to indicate that hostage takers prefer not to take U.S. or UK hostages—almost certainly because they understand that they will not receive ransoms. (Cohen, 2012, p. 6)

Patrick T. Brandt, Justin George, and Todd Sandler, three professors at the University of Texas at Dallas, set out to test whether Cohen's statement was supported by empirical evidence. Specifically, they wanted to

> ascertain how, if at all, the recent no-concession policy of the United States and the United Kingdom has changed the abductions of Americans and British people by concession-seeking terrorists. Is it true that these terrorists have increasingly abducted hostages from known concession-granting [ransom-paying] countries—i.e., Austria, Belgium, Canada, France, Germany, Italy, Netherlands, Spain, Sweden, and Switzerland—which we call the "Concessionaires"? (Brandt, George, and Sandler, 2016, p. 42)

Brandt, George, and Sandler apply some sophisticated techniques of quantitative analysis (a Bayesian Poisson change-point model) to kidnapping incidents associated with three cohorts of countries that differ in their frequency of granting concessions. The analysis indicates that countries are better off not conceding to ransom or other requests (such as the release of prisoners): "Depending on the cohort of countries during 2001–2013, terrorist negotiation successes encouraged 64% to 87% more kidnappings." The findings also held "for 1978–2013, during which these negotiation successes encouraged 26% to 57% more kidnappings" (Brandt, George, and Sandler, 2016, p. 41). (*Negotiation success*, as used by the authors, refers to the kidnappers' success in obtaining concessions rather than negotiations leading to the hostages' safe release.)

The analysts divide the responding countries into three groups: the United States and United Kingdom (which advertise no-ransom policies), the European Union (minus the United Kingdom), and the concessionaire countries whose governments reportedly pay ransoms (Austria, Belgium, Canada, France, Germany, Italy, the Netherlands, Spain, Sweden, and Switzerland).

The historical records of the three groups differ. Between 1978 and 2000, concessions were made in 23.1 percent of the cases where U.S. nationals were held hostage and in 10.9 percent of the cases where UK nationals were held. The authors point out that the United States held truer to its no-concessions policy after 2001. Between 2001 and 2013, concessions were made in only 10.7 percent of the cases involving U.S. nationals and in 10.4 percent of the cases involving UK nationals. The higher number of U.S. cases involving concessions in the earlier period may reflect concessions made by other countries to obtain the release of American hostages and concessions secretly made by the U.S. government, in violation of its own policy, to obtain the release of American hostages kidnapped in Lebanon during the 1980s.

Concessions were made in 18.8 percent of the cases involving European Union citizens between 1978 and 2000 and in 21.1 percent of the cases between 2001 and 2013. The concessionaire countries resolved 20.2 percent of the cases involving their nationals in the 1978–2000 period and 23.8 percent of those in the 2001–2013 period. If terrorists were to read this analysis, they would conclude that nationals of the concessionaire countries are preferred targets, assuming, of course, that obtaining ransoms or other concessions is their paramount objective.

The authors also looked at the monthly rate of kidnappings experienced by the nationals of the three groups in the pre-2001 period and in the 2001–2013 period to identify the effect that terrorist negotiating successes have on the frequency of further kidnappings. They concluded that terrorist successes in obtaining concessions result in more hostages being abducted, because of the terrorists' anticipated future payoffs. By granting concessions, the European Union after 2006 and the concessionaire countries after 2008 increased the median rate of kidnappings of their citizens by 80 percent and 72 percent, respectively.

This finding would seem to confirm the observation resulting from earlier research that a demonstrated willingness to pay ransom encourages further kidnappings. Certainly, this was the case in Argentina in the early 1970s and subsequently in Lebanon and Colombia.

In contrast, the authors argue that, by adhering to a no-ransom policy, the United States and the United Kingdom were able to "eliminate a marginal increase in the median rate of kidnappings of their citizens by 87% for 2001–2013"—in other words, fewer kidnappings occurred than would have been the case under a different

> Brandt, George, and Sandler concluded that terrorist successes in obtaining concessions result in more hostages being abducted, because of the terrorists' anticipated future payoffs.

policy regime (Brandt, George, and Sandler, 2016, p. 51). However, the authors go on to warn that this does not mean, as suggested by Undersecretary Cohen, that U.S. and UK citizens will not be taken hostage:

> Unfortunately, U.S. and UK citizens will still be taken hostage because of terrorists' grievances and their anticipated media attention from such abductions. Nevertheless, limiting an increase in the median rate of abductions is a huge benefit, given the marginal effects on future kidnappings identified here, and greatly supports the continuation of these countries' no-concession policy. (Brandt, George, and Sandler, 2016, p. 51)

The Brandt, George, and Sandler study contradicts the Loertscher and Milton study in its overall conclusion about the efficacy of a no-ransom policy and its assumption that kidnappers even know the nationality of their targets prior to the kidnapping. Anecdotal evidence also suggests that a number of those kidnapped in the post-2001 period were taken by al Qaeda kidnappers operating in former French North Africa, where European nationals were simply easier targets than U.S. or UK nationals. Further detailed analysis is required to reconcile the different findings.

2017 New America Study

The third analysis, carried out by Christopher Mellon, Peter Bergen, and David Sterman at New America, looked at the cases of 1,185 Western hostages held by terrorist, militant, and pirate organizations between 2001 and 2016 (Mellon, Bergen, and Sterman, 2017). Their conclusions are consistent with the findings of Loertscher and Milton

and earlier RAND research. The following are among their key findings (quoted directly):

- Hostages from European countries known to pay ransoms are more likely to be released.
- Citizens of countries that make concessions such as ransom payments do not appear to be kidnapped at disproportionately high rates. There is no clear link between a nation's ransom policy and the number of its citizens taken hostage.
- Eight out of 10 [European Union] hostages held by jihadist terrorist groups were freed compared to one in four for the United States and one in three for the United Kingdom.
- Rescue operations are dangerous and often result in hostage deaths.[6]
- The French government's efforts to move toward a no-concessions policy in 2010 led to an increase in hostage deaths. (Mellon, Bergen, and Sterman, 2017, pp. 3–5)

The authors underscore that their research produced two primary conclusions: "First, countries that do not make concessions experience far worse outcomes for their kidnapped citizens than countries that do. Second, there is no evidence that American and British citizens are more protected than other Westerners by the refusal of their governments to make concessions" (Mellon, Bergen, and Sterman, 2017, p. 13). This is contrary to the findings of the Brandt, George, and Sanders study but consistent with RAND's earlier research and with the Loertscher and Milton study.

Conclusions

There is little historical evidence to support the contention that a no-concessions policy reduces kidnappings, although the recent sophisticated quantitative analysis carried out by Brandt, George, and Sanders argues that adhering to a no-ransom policy reduces the number of kidnappings that might otherwise have been anticipated. In other words, without a declared no-ransom policy, things would have been worse. The findings are robust, but other circumstances that may affect the results merit a much closer look. Regardless of the questionable efficacy of a no-concessions policy as a deterrent, this does not mean that it should be abandoned, because it serves other policy objectives.

Whether making concessions encourages further kidnappings is a more complicated matter. Some evidence suggests that it does. The willingness of the government of Brazil to release prisoners in the early kidnappings invited repetition. The willingness of corporations in Argentina to pay ransoms for kidnapped executives set off a wave of kidnappings and escalating ransom demands and appears to have encouraged this tactic as a routine way for terrorist organizations to finance their operations. The Brandt, George, and Sanders study also supports the idea that advertised payment of ransoms encourages further abductions.

At the same time, kidnappings also continued in Uruguay, which adopted a no-concessions policy; many of the kidnappings there were for publicity purposes and involved no demands. Outlawing ransom payments, which several countries attempted to do, did not result in discernible declines in kidnappings.

> Regardless of the questionable efficacy of a no-concessions policy as a deterrent, this does not mean that it should be abandoned, because it serves other policy objectives.

The U.S. no-concessions policy has not produced any noticeable decline in the number of kidnappings of Americans. However, as with all deterrent policies, it can be argued that more kidnappings might have occurred had the United States routinely made concessions. This is the conclusion of Brandt, George, and Sanders.

National policies on concessions appear to have little effect on the nationalities of those who are targeted by kidnappers. This is the conclusion of the RAND research, and it is reinforced by the findings of Loertscher and Milton and of Mellon, Bergen, and Sterman. However, the latter two studies indicate that national policies do appear to have an effect on the outcome of kidnapping episodes. Hostages from nations that publicly adhere to no-concessions policies appear to be held longer and are more often killed by their captors than hostages of nations

A single database devoted to and designed specifically for abductions could provide the foundation for the analysis of trends, tactics, effects of policy, and other issues.

that reportedly pay ransoms, although other factors may provide part of the explanation.

While the absence of empirical evidence that a no-concessions policy is a deterrent does not mean that the policy necessarily should be abandoned, it does make it more difficult for the United States to persuade other governments that they should adopt similar policies. This is a significant finding as the United States tries to persuade other governments to adopt no-concessions policies. It may need to advance other arguments.

The apprehension of kidnappers and the destruction of kidnapping gangs appear to be the most powerful factors in reducing kidnappings.

Further Research

Several lines of additional inquiry have already been indicated. One major shortcoming is simply the paucity of good data. Calculating the total number of kidnappings worldwide would be extremely difficult. Such crime statistics, where available, reflect different definitions. Only very rough estimates would be possible.

More doable, but still lacking, is a good database of abductions of foreign nationals. The database created by START at the University of Maryland; the ITERATE (International Terrorism: Attributes of Terrorist Events) database at Duke University; the database used by Loertscher and Milton; the database used by Brandt, George, and Sandler; the Mellon, Bergen, and Sterman study; and information compiled by Humanitarian Outcomes are excellent sources, but all of them lack many details.[7] Some of these details will be known only to those involved in the negotiations, but a concerted effort can be made to fill in some of the blanks.

Some of the private consultancies that provided assistance to families and corporations faced with kidnappings developed databases detailing demands, negotiating tactics, durations of captivity, final settlements, outcomes, and other elements of information useful to their practice. It would be possible to design a properly formatted framework for entries and then populate it. A single database devoted to and designed specifically for abductions could provide the foundation for the analysis of trends, tactics, effects of policy, and other issues.

Another key issue is the importance of ransom as a source of financing for terrorist organizations. We do not have good information on ransom payments—amounts demanded, negotiating methods, amounts paid, and so forth. These data and expertise in the subject reside largely in the private sector. Private kidnapping consultants have most of the experience. In some cases, insurance companies and consulting firms have collected this information, but the state of these private efforts today is not known.

If governments are to follow no-concessions policies and not abandon their nationals, the options seem to be rescue or diplomatic persuasion. We need to think more creatively about what might be done to secure the release of hostages without inviting more kidnappings by making concessions. Often, the answer has turned out to be allowing others to make concessions. As mentioned previously, the no-ransom policy of the United States applies to the government of the United States, which discourages, but does not interfere with, concessions made by other governments or ransom negotiations by private parties.

In 2014, President Obama ordered a review of how the U.S. government handles hostage situations. This led to a new Presidential Policy Directive in 2015 that made organizational changes aimed at improving government coordination and relations with hostage families. The policy directive created a Hostage Response Group that will recommend hostage recovery options and strategies to the president, a Hostage Recovery Fusion Cell that serves as the U.S. government's dedicated interagency coordinating body for the recovery of U.S. nationals held hostage abroad, a special envoy for hostage affairs to coordinate diplomatic efforts, and a family engagement coordinator to work and communicate with the families of hostages (White House, 2015).

In the more than two years since the policy directive, terrorists have continued to kidnap U.S. citizens. Most of those have been released, which was always the case. If not the U.S. government, someone has negotiated with the kidnappers, and it is likely that concessions, including the payment of ransom, have been made in some cases. There may be other cases in which intermediaries with influence over the hostage holders have been able to persuade them that it is in their interest to release their captives. It would be useful to examine these cases in detail to distill lessons learned that might be applied to other cases.

Appendix. A Summary of RAND's Early Research on Hostage-Taking

From 1973 to the end of the decade, RAND researchers looked at the trajectory of hostage-taking in several countries where terrorist groups had been active, and that research is summarized in this appendix. A complete list of RAND's unclassified publications on kidnapping is provided in the bibliography, and although some of the research remains unpublished, it is summarized here.

Brazil. The first successful modern-era kidnapping of a diplomat occurred in Brazil in September 1969, when urban guerrillas abducted the U.S. ambassador and demanded that the government of Brazil release 15 imprisoned comrades. The government complied, and the ambassador was released. That success inspired the kidnapping of the Japanese consul general in Sao Paulo in February 1970. The Brazilian government again complied with the kidnappers' demands. In June 1970, the German ambassador was kidnapped. The Brazilian government again complied, and 40 prisoners were released. In December, the Swiss ambassador was abducted. The government of Brazil signaled its willingness to comply, and ultimately 70 prisoners were released in return for the safe release of the ambassador. During this same period, Brazil's urban guerrillas attempted several other kidnappings, including that of the U.S. consul general in Porto Alegre. In addition, several kidnapping plots were discovered and thwarted by the authorities.

The pattern suggests that the Brazilian government's advertised willingness to meet the demands of terrorist kidnappers invited further attempts and escalating demands. However, the government followed each prisoner release with a massive crackdown on the groups involved. For example, 8,000 people were reportedly arrested at the time of the Swiss ambassador's kidnapping. The death penalty was restored, and other penalties for terrorist-related crimes were increased. At the same time, Brazil's economy improved and the popular uprising the urban guerrillas hoped to inspire never occurred. Arbitrary arrests and the use of torture in interrogations were common. Tactically, Brazil's terrorist groups had won every negotiation. Strategically, they lost the war.

Uruguay. Uruguay's urban guerillas, the Tupamaros, had begun kidnapping local politicians even before Brazil's groups began kidnapping foreign diplomats. In the beginning, the Tupamaros used the kidnappings as publicity stunts to extract information about corruption and political connections that they would release to embarrass the government, although they also made demands for ransom payments in some cases.

In July 1970, the Tupamaros kidnapped a U.S. public safety adviser. At the same time, they kidnapped the Brazilian consul general, and one week later, they kidnapped a U.S. agricultural adviser. In return for the release of their hostages, they demanded the release of 150 prisoners. The government of Uruguay took a hard line and refused to negotiate, instead launching a massive manhunt for the kidnappers. In response, the Tupamaros killed the public safety adviser. The Brazilian diplomat was held for six months, then released, reportedly after his family paid a ransom. The Tupamaros released the agricultural adviser seven months later, after he suffered a heart attack.

By that time, the Tupamaros also held the British ambassador, whom they had kidnapped in January 1971. The Uruguayan government continued to reject the kidnappers' demands, and the ambassador was held captive for eight months before being released without the release of any prisoners. The case was viewed as a victory for the no-concessions policy, which the British government has adhered to ever since. Upon the ambassador's release, however, the Tupamaros announced that they had given him an amnesty and that, because 106 of their comrades had escaped from prison just a few days earlier, there was no longer any need to hold him hostage. Later, in 2002, a British newspaper reported that the ambassador's release had, in fact, been the result of a secret negotiation and a payment of £42,000 (about $880,000 in 2016 U.S. dollars), which had been brokered by Salvador Allende, the Marxist president of Chile at the time (Day, 2002).

As in Brazil, the kidnappings in Uruguay provoked a massive crackdown on the Tupamaros, including the employment of death squads, arbitrary arrests, and the routine use of torture as the armed forces played a growing role in governing the country. By mid-1972, the Tupamaros had been crushed, and there were no further kidnappings.

Argentina. The tactic of kidnapping spread to Argentina in the early 1970s. Like Uruguay, the Argentine government adopted a no-concessions policy. Although Argentina also prohibited private ransom payments, the government rarely interfered with private negotiations.

Secret payments of ransom had been made in some of the Uruguayan kidnappings. Latin America's kidnappers worried that ransom kidnapping—as opposed to demands for the publication of manifestos or the release of prisoners—would tarnish the urban guerrillas' image, making them appear to be no different from common criminals.

The change in terrorist policy in Argentina came about in two steps. In a May 1971 kidnapping of corporate executives, Argentina's urban guerrillas demanded that the corporation fund philanthropic enterprises, such as the distribution of food in poor neighborhoods, in exchange for the release of the hostages. The corporation complied.

This led to another kidnapping, and the kidnappers this time demanded that the government release prisoners and that the corporation rehire workers who had been fired in a labor dispute and pay $1 million for the distribution of shoes and school supplies to children in poor areas. The government rejected the demands and launched a search for the kidnappers' hideout. The hostage was killed during the rescue attempt. Then, in a 1972 kidnapping, the kidnappers demanded a cash ransom, which was paid.

Kidnappings proliferated, and ransom demands quickly escalated into the millions, giving rise to the emergence of kidnap-and-ransom insurance coverage. The kidnappings continued until the mid-1970s, when brutal repression finally destroyed the terrorist groups (Jenkins, 1984b).

Turkey. Like Uruguay and Argentina, Turkey also adopted a no-concessions policy when faced with its first terrorist kidnappings in the early 1970s. Some hostages were released without concessions being made, while others were murdered by their captors or killed during rescue attempts. A massive crackdown on the groups responsible ended the kidnappings.

Germany. In the early 1970s, Germany had to deal with kidnappings of German diplomats in Guatemala, Brazil, and Spain, and later with kidnappings by German terrorist groups operating in Germany. In the cases of abduction of German diplomats abroad, the German government, like the U.S. government, urged local governments to do whatever was necessary to bring about the release of the hostages. The Guatemalan government refused to release prisoners, and the German ambassador was murdered. Later that year, Brazil agreed to release prisoners, and the ambassador was released. In Spain, Basque separatists who kidnapped the German consul general demanded leniency for six of their comrades who were on trial. A secret deal was struck, and the kidnappers released their hostage. The court sentenced the six men to death, but the head of state, Francisco Franco, promptly commuted their sentences to long prison terms.

In 1975, members of the June 2 Group, a German terrorist organization, kidnapped a candidate for mayor of Berlin and demanded the release of two prisoners. Germany agreed, and after the prisoners were flown out of the country, the mayor, who had won the election while in captivity, was released. This success may have encouraged the Red Army Faction (RAF), another German terrorist group, to kidnap the head of the Confederation of German Employers' Associations and demand the release of four RAF leaders. In a supporting operation, Palestinian terrorists hijacked a Lufthansa airliner and flew it to Mogadishu. In this case, the German government rejected the kidnappers' demands, and a team of German commandos flew to Mogadishu and rescued the hostages in a daring assault. Disheartened by the German government's refusal to consider their release and news of the commandos' successful rescue, three of the four prisoners whose release was demanded committed suicide. In retaliation, the kidnappers murdered their captive. With the deaths of their leaders, however, the number of German terrorists declined, and there were no further kidnappings.

Italy. Ransom kidnappings by criminal gangs were common in Italy in the 1970s. Between 1970 and 1982, there were 487 such incidents. In response, the government outlawed the payment of ransom, froze bank accounts in some cases, and prohibited Italian insurance companies from issuing kidnap-and-ransom insurance. Some of these measures were intended to discourage families from secret negotiations, but if a family notified and worked with the authorities, ransoms could still be negotiated. Other targets of the prohibitions were attempts by some wealthy families to orchestrate fake kidnappings and ransom payments to evade taxes and currency controls.

The same period saw 25 politically motivated kidnappings, two by right-wing extremists and 23 by left-wing extremists, including 17 kidnappings by the Red Brigades. Emulating South America's urban guerrillas, the Red Brigades kidnapped to gain publicity; create political crises; make political demands; punish corporate officials for "anti-proletarian activities"; and, in two cases, obtain funding for further operations. In 1978, the group kidnapped former Prime Minister Aldo Moro and demanded the release of 13 comrades who were on trial. When the government rejected the group's demands, Moro was murdered.

In early 1981, the group struck again, carrying out a series of four kidnappings aimed at both political and corporate figures and the brother of an imprisoned Red Brigades member who had renounced the group while in jail. The kidnappers of a Montedison executive made no demands but instead announced that he had been sentenced to death, and he was killed, as was the brother of a Red Brigades member who had turned on the group.[8] Later in 1981, the same Venice column that had kidnapped and killed the Montedison executive kidnapped a U.S. general. This was the group's first abduction of a foreign national. The Italian government refused to meet the kidnappers' demands, and there was considerable concern that they would kill the general (because they had killed the Montedison executive), but Italian commandos rescued him. By this time, the group was falling apart due to arrests and defections, and there were no further political kidnappings (Pisano, 1984).

Lebanon. By the late 1970s, most of Latin America's urban guerrilla groups had been destroyed, although guerrilla campaigns continued in Central America and Colombia, which saw a growing volume of ransom kidnappings by the surviving groups and by ordinary gangs. Terrorists in Germany and Italy carried out some dramatic kidnappings in the 1970s and early 1980s, but by the mid-1980s, these groups had also declined. Europe's two most persistent terrorist organizations, the Provisional Wing of the Irish Republican Army and the Basque separatist ETA (Euskadi Ta Askatasuna), rarely kidnapped, for reasons that had more to do with their operational codes than with government policy. By the mid-1980s, Lebanon had become the main theater of political kidnappings.

Many of the kidnappings in Lebanon were carried out by criminal gangs taking advantage of the chaos created by the country's civil war, which began in 1975, but most of the kidnappings of foreign nationals were carried out by Shia guerrilla groups. Their motives varied. Raising cash was a factor in some cases, but some of the kidnappings of foreigners were connected with political demands—in particular, efforts to bring about the release of Shia prisoners held in Kuwait. Ordinary criminal groups also kidnapped hostages and sold them to the political groups.

By 1985, 36 Americans had been kidnapped in Lebanon, along with 15 French citizens, 11 UK citizens, four nationals of the Soviet Union, three Spanish citizens, two

Germans, and a mix of other Europeans (Jenkins and Wright, 1987). (More than 2,000 Lebanese were kidnapped during the same period.) Government policies varied. The United States and the United Kingdom reiterated their no-concessions policies—which were by now considered in government circles to be a deterrent, although there was no detailed analysis that I am aware of. The French, Germans, and other Europeans were suspected of secretly negotiating ransoms. Their nationals came home, while the U.S. and UK nationals were held for years.

The 1985 kidnapping of four Soviet diplomats in Beirut is often held up as an example of an effective hardline response. One of the diplomats was murdered during the abduction, and according to the popular version of events, the three others were released after Soviet agents grabbed a relative of the leader of the group responsible for the kidnapping, cut off his ear (various versions mention different parts of his anatomy), and sent it to the kidnappers with a warning that other parts would be cut off if the hostages were not released. This story had considerable appeal in the United States, particularly among those who grudgingly admired tough Soviet methods for handling hostage incidents.

At a meeting in Moscow several years later, Soviet officials offered me an entirely different version of the incident. According to them, when the kidnapping occurred, the Soviet government immediately evacuated the rest of its diplomatic staff from Lebanon and dispatched a special emissary to Damascus and Beirut. At Soviet urging, the Syrian government and Sheikh Said Shabaan, the leader of a Sunni fundamentalist group the Syrians then had under siege and on whose behalf the kidnapping had been carried out, reached an accord and halted the fighting that was going on between Syrian government forces and the group. (Other sources told me earlier that, under Soviet pressure, Syria was obliged to lift its siege of Shabaan's forces in Lebanon.) Shabaan then came to Damascus under a guarantee of safe conduct. In Damascus, Shabaan was pressured by the Iranians, his principal financial backers, to virtually capitulate. The fighting ended, and the three diplomats were returned safely. It was not the threatened severance of further body parts but behind-the-scenes diplomacy that brought the Soviet hostages home (Jenkins, 1989).

Meanwhile, the United States undermined its own announced no-concessions policy by secretly agreeing to sell arms to Iran in return for Iran's assistance in bringing about the release of American hostages. In accordance with this deal, some American hostages were released, one at a time; however, as some came out, the terrorists kidnapped others, giving them a constant "bank account" of hostages. The American-Iranian arrangement ended when it was revealed in the news media in late 1986, creating an embarrassing scandal for the Reagan administration.[9]

United States. The United States has a long and rich history of dealing with hostage situations, going back to the 18th century, when U.S. merchant vessels sailing in the Mediterranean were attacked by pirates from the Barbary Coast, and their crews were held for ransom. The only domestic political kidnapping in the modern era is that of Patricia Hearst, kidnapped in 1974 by members of a group calling itself the Symbionese Liberation Army. In return for her release, the group demanded that the Hearst family distribute $4 million worth of food to the needy, which the U.S. government did not try to prohibit.

The earlier 20th-century history of kidnapping may be more instructive. During the 1920s and 1930s, ransom kidnappings by criminal gangs and amateur criminals were not uncommon. That began to change with the kidnapping of the infant son of Charles Lindbergh. The death of the child shocked the nation and led to a number of changes in the way kidnappings were handled. Bringing kidnap victims across state lines became a federal crime; after 48 hours, then 24 hours, and later without delay, federal authorities could intervene on the assumption that the victim may have been carried across state lines. That made kidnappings a federal matter. The government made no attempt to interfere with negotiations or payment of ransom. Instead, the newly created FBI used the communications to gain information about the kidnappers.

This improved apprehension rates. Convictions were easy—jury members saw kidnappers as villains in a human drama and readily came back with guilty verdicts. Penalties were stiffened. To be convicted of a kidnapping meant life behind bars, if not a death sentence. Professional criminals considered kidnapping too risky, leaving the crime to amateurs, who were easily caught. Apprehension rates approached 100 percent. As a result, ransom kidnapping plummeted and today remains a comparatively rare crime, confined to settling accounts in drug deals gone bad or occurring in a few unassimilated immigrant communities (Gallagher, 1984).

Notes

[1] A complete list of RAND's unclassified publications on kidnapping, plus some important works by others, is provided in the bibliography. Some of RAND's original work remains unpublished and cannot be included.

[2] Jenkins did not like the title; the book addressed kidnapping more broadly, but the publisher insisted on having "terrorism" on the cover of the book.

[3] The RAND reports deriving from this research, as well as important works by others, are included in the bibliography.

[4] In 1995, President Bill Clinton signed Executive Order 12947, prohibiting "financial, material, or technological support" to persons who committed or pose a significant risk of committing violence. The original order designated 12 organizations that threatened the Middle East peace process. President Clinton expanded the list to include Osama bin Laden and his organization in 1998. Meanwhile, the U.S. Congress passed legislation in 1996 requiring the Department of State to identify foreign terrorist organizations and imposed sanctions on dealings with them. See Executive Order 12947, 1995.

[5] Since 1994, the U.S. Criminal Code outlaws providing material support when knowing or intending that it will be used to commit terrorist offenses (18 U.S.C. 2339A) or providing material support to designated terrorist groups (18 U.S.C. 2339B). The definition of *material support* has been broadened to encompass a broad range of tangible and intangible assistance, including funding and fundraising, providing goods or services, recruiting, volunteering for service, providing technical expertise or other knowledge, assisting in propaganda, and otherwise aiding any individuals or organizations engaged in terrorist activity. It is the most frequently used statute in terrorist-related prosecutions. The statute does not specifically mention the payment of ransom, however. Family members of James Foley, who was kidnapped and later killed by ISIS, reportedly were threatened by the FBI that they could be prosecuted for paying a ransom to ISIS in exchange for their son. It is debatable whether a court would define ransom payments, which are made under duress, as material support—or that a jury would convict on those grounds. However, while families may claim a duress defense, others involved—for example, intermediaries who assist in such negotiations and in making a ransom payment—might not be able to do so.

[6] Earlier RAND research showed that hostages may die during the abduction, may die attempting to escape, may be murdered by their captors or die of illness or mistreatment during their captivity, or may be killed during a rescue attempt. Of these four possibilities, being killed during the rescue attempt accounted for 79 percent of the hostage fatalities. See Jenkins, Johnson, and Ronfeldt, 1977.

[7] Humanitarian Outcomes is a team of specialist consultants providing research and policy advice for humanitarian aid agencies and donor governments. For the sources described, see the bibliography.

[8] As a consultant to Montedison, I was personally involved in the case.

[9] During this period, I served as a consultant to Catholic Relief Services, which was dealing with the kidnapping of Father Martin Jenco in Lebanon, and later as a consultant to the Church of England in the matter of the British hostages in Lebanon. In this capacity, I served as an informal liaison between these organizations and U.S. government officials.

Bibliography

Bass, Gail, Brian M. Jenkins, Konrad Kellen, David Ronfeldt, and Joyce Peterson, *Options for U.S. Policy on Terrorism*, Santa Monica, Calif.: RAND Corporation, R-2764-RC, 1981. As of September 27, 2017:
https://www.rand.org/pubs/reports/R2764.html

Brandt, Patrick T., Justin George, and Todd Sandler, "Why Concessions Should Not Be Made to Terrorist Kidnappers," *European Journal of Political Economy*, Vol. 44, September 2016, pp. 41–52. As of September 27, 2017:
http://www.sciencedirect.com/science/article/pii/S0176268016300143

Callimachi, Rukmini, "Paying Ransoms, Europe Bankrolls Qaeda Terror," *New York Times*, July 29, 2014. As of September 27, 2017:
https://www.nytimes.com/2014/07/30/world/africa/ransoming-citizens-europe-becomes-al-qaedas-patron.html

Cohen, David S., "Kidnapping for Ransom: The Growing Terrorism Financing Challenge," transcript, London: Chatham House, October 5, 2012. As of September 27, 2017:
https://www.chathamhouse.org/sites/files/chathamhouse/public/Meetings/Meeting%20Transcripts/051012Cohen.pdf

Day, Peter, "Heath's Secret Deal to Free Ambassador," *The Telegraph,* January 1, 2002.

Dutton, Yvonne M., "Funding Terrorism: The Problem of Ransom Payments," *San Diego Law Review*, Vol. 53, 2016, pp. 335–367.

Executive Order 12947, Prohibiting Transactions with Terrorists Who Threaten to Disrupt the Middle East Peace Process, 60 *Federal Register* 5079, January 25, 1995.

Foster, Peter, "Did Qatar Pay Ransom for Release of U.S. Journalist Peter Theo Curtis?" *The Telegraph,* August 25, 2014.

Gallagher, Richard J., "Kidnapping in the United States and the Development of the Federal Kidnapping Statute," in Brian Michael Jenkins, ed., *Terrorism and Personal Protection,* Boston, Mass.: Butterworth-Heinemann, 1984, pp. 129–145.

Jenkins, Brian Michael, *International Terrorism: A New Kind of Warfare,* Santa Monica, Calif.: RAND Corporation, P-5261, 1974a. As of September 27, 2017:
https://www.rand.org/pubs/papers/P5261.html

———, *Should Corporations Be Prevented from Paying Ransom,* Santa Monica, Calif.: RAND Corporation, P-5291, 1974b. As of September 27, 2017:
https://www.rand.org/pubs/papers/P5291.html

———, *Terrorism and Kidnapping,* Santa Monica, Calif.: RAND Corporation, P-5255, 1974c. As of September 27, 2017:
https://www.rand.org/pubs/papers/P5255.html

———, *Hostage Survival: Some Preliminary Observations,* Santa Monica, Calif.: RAND Corporation, P-5627, 1976. As of September 27, 2017:
https://www.rand.org/pubs/papers/P5627.html

———, *Terrorists Seize Hostages in Arcadia: Laconia Commandos on Alert: A Scenario for Simulation in Negotiations with Terrorists Holding Hostages,* Santa Monica, Calif.: RAND Corporation, P-6339, 1979. As of September 27, 2017:
https://www.rand.org/pubs/papers/P6339.html

———, *Embassies Under Siege: A Review of 48 Embassy Takeovers, 1971–1980,* Santa Monica, Calif.: RAND Corporation, R-2651-RC, 1981. As of September 27, 2017:
https://www.rand.org/pubs/reports/R2651.html

———, *Diplomats on the Front Line,* Santa Monica, Calif.: RAND Corporation, P-6749, 1982a. As of September 27, 2017:
https://www.rand.org/pubs/papers/P6749.html

———, *Talking to Terrorists,* Santa Monica, Calif.: RAND Corporation, P-6750, 1982b. As of September 27, 2017:
https://www.rand.org/pubs/papers/P6750.html

———, ed., *Terrorism and Personal Protection,* Boston, Mass.: Butterworth-Heinemann, November 1984a.

———, "The Payment of Ransom," in Brian M. Jenkins, ed., *Terrorism and Personal Protection,* Boston, Mass.: Butterworth-Heinemann, November 1984b, pp. 222–231.

———, *The Possibility of Soviet-American Cooperation Against Terrorism,* Santa Monica, Calif.: RAND Corporation, P-7541, 1989. As of September 27, 2017:
https://www.rand.org/pubs/papers/P7541.html

———, *Getting the Hostages Out: Who Turns the Key?* Santa Monica, Calif.: RAND Corporation, P-7647, 1990. As of September 27, 2017:
https://www.rand.org/pubs/papers/P7647.html

———, "Introduction," in Meg Williams, Ed Williams, John Yourston, Patty Ogilvey, Andrew Price, and Eva Molyneux, *Kidnapping in Iraq: April 2004–February 2005,* London: Olive Security (UK) Limited, 2006, pp. 4–10.

———, "Why the U.S. Swaps Prisoners but Doesn't Pay Ransom," *The Hill,* August 29, 2014.

Jenkins, Brian, Janera Johnson, and David Ronfeldt, *Numbered Lives: Some Statistical Observations from 77 International Hostage Episodes,* Santa Monica, Calif.: RAND Corporation, P-5905, 1977. As of September 27, 2017:
https://www.rand.org/pubs/papers/P5905.html

Jenkins, Brian, David Ronfeldt, and Helen Turin, *Dealing with Political Kidnapping: Executive Summary,* Santa Monica, Calif.: RAND Corporation, R-1857/1-DOS/ARPA, 1976.

Jenkins, Brian, and Ralph Strauch, *Assessment of Current U.S. Policy on Kidnapping of Diplomats and Policy Alternatives,* Santa Monica, Calif.: RAND Corporation, WN-8934-DOS/ARPA, 1975.

Jenkins, Brian Michael, Meg Williams, and Ed Williams, "Iraq Kidnapping Strategically Effective," *Chicago Tribune,* April 29, 2005. As of September 27, 2017:
http://articles.chicagotribune.com/2005-04-29/
news/0504290168_1_kidnapping-olive-security-hostages

Jenkins, Brian Michael, and Robin Wright, "The Kidnappings in Lebanon," *TVI Report,* Vol. 7, No. 4, 1987.

Krahenbuhl, Margaret, *Political Kidnappings in Turkey, 1971–1972,* Santa Monica, Calif.: RAND Corporation, R-2105-DOS/ARPA, 1977. As of September 27, 2017:
https://www.rand.org/pubs/reports/R2105.html

Lion, Ed, "Two Men Paid $21,600 by the Church of England," *UPI,* January 11, 1988. As of September 27, 2017:
http://www.upi.com/Archives/1988/01/11/
Two-men-paid-21600-by-the-Church-of-England/3825568875600/

Loertscher, Seth, and Daniel Milton, *Held Hostage: Analyses of Kidnapping Across Time and Among Jihadist Organizations,* West Point, N.Y.: Combating Terrorism Center at West Point, United States Military Academy, 2015.

Mellon, Christopher, Peter Bergen, and David Sterman, *To Pay or Not to Pay Ransom? An Examination of Western Hostage Policies,* Washington, D.C.: New America, January 2017. As of September 27, 2017:
https://na-production.s3.amazonaws.com/documents/
hostage-paper-final.pdf

Meyer, Josh, "Why the G8 Pact to Stop Paying Terrorist Ransoms Probably Won't Work—and Isn't Even Such a Great Idea," *Quartz,* June 19, 2013. As of September 27, 2017:
https://qz.com/95618/why-the-g8-pact-to-stop-paying-terrorist-
ransoms-probably-wont-work-and-isnt-even-such-a-great-idea/

National Consortium for the Study of Terrorism and Responses to Terrorism, Global Terrorism Database, College Park, Md.: University of Maryland, undated. As of September 27, 2017:
http://www.start.umd.edu/gtd/

Osorio, Carlos, and Marianna Enamoneta, "To Save Dan Mitrione Nixon Administration Urged Death Threats for Uruguayan Prisoners," *National Security Archive,* Washington, D.C., August 11, 2010.

Pisano, Vittorfranco S., "The Italian Experience," in Brian Michael Jenkins, ed., *Terrorism and Personal Protection,* Boston, Mass.: Butterworth-Heinemann, 1984, pp. 64–87.

Randazza, Marc J., "Getting to Yes with Terrorists," *Michigan State Law Review,* Vol. 2002, 2002, pp. 823–834.

Ronfeldt, David, *The Mitrione Kidnapping in Uruguay,* Santa Monica, Calif.: RAND Corporation, N-1571-DOS/DARPA/RC, 1987. As of September 27, 2017:
https://www.rand.org/pubs/notes/N1571.html

Shortland, Anja, and Tom Keatinge, *Closing the Gap: Assessing the Responses to Terrorist-Related Kidnap-for-Ransom,* London: Royal United Services Institute, September 12, 2017. As of September 27, 2017:
https://rusi.org/publication/occasional-papers/
closing-gap-assessing-responses-terrorist-related-kidnap-ransom

START—*See* National Consortium for the Study of Terrorism and Responses to Terrorism.

United States Code, Title 18, Section 2339A, Providing Material Support to Terrorists.

United States Code, Title 18, Section 2339B, Providing Material Support or Resources to Designated Foreign Terrorist Organizations.

U.S. Department of State, "7 FAM 1820, Hostage Taking and Kidnappings," *Foreign Affairs Manual and Handbook,* Washington, D.C., July 26, 2006.

Wainstein, Eleanor S., *The Cross and Laporte Kidnappings, Montreal, October 1970,* Santa Monica, Calif.: RAND Corporation, R-1986/1-DOS/ARPA, 1977. As of September 27, 2017:
https://www.rand.org/pubs/reports/R1986z1.html

White House, *Hostage Recovery Activities,* Presidential Policy Directive 30, June 24, 2015. As of September 27, 2017:
https://obamawhitehouse.archives.gov/the-press-office/2015/06/24/
presidential-policy-directive-hostage-recovery-activities

About the Author

Brian Michael Jenkins, senior adviser to the president of the RAND Corporation, is the author of numerous reports, articles, and testimonies on terrorism-related topics. He formerly served as chair of the Political Science Department at RAND. On the occasion of the ten-year anniversary of 9/11, Jenkins initiated a RAND effort to take stock of America's policy reactions and give thoughtful consideration to future strategy. That effort is presented in *The Long Shadow of 9/11: America's Response to Terrorism* (Brian Michael Jenkins and John Paul Godges, eds., 2011).

Commissioned in the infantry, Jenkins became a paratrooper and a captain in the Green Berets. He is a decorated combat veteran, having served in the Seventh Special Forces Group in the Dominican Republic and with the Fifth Special Forces Group in Vietnam. He returned to Vietnam as a member of the Long Range Planning Task Group and received the Department of the Army's highest award for his service. In 1996, President Clinton appointed Jenkins to the White House Commission on Aviation Safety and Security. From 1999 to 2000, he served as adviser to the National Commission on Terrorism and in 2000 was appointed to the U.S. Comptroller General's Advisory Board. He is a research associate at the Mineta Transportation Institute, where he directs the continuing research on protecting surface transportation against terrorist attacks.